Crypto

Understanding crypto, blockchains and what they are and how they are worth value

About

A passionate Gen Xer with a thirst for knowledge, the author embarked on a journey to demystify the complexities of cryptocurrency and blockchains after grappling with the concept of Bitcoin. Driven by a desire to empower others with understanding and clarity, they delved deep into the intricacies of digital currencies, ultimately crafting this insightful guide. With a relatable perspective and a commitment to helping others navigate the digital financial landscape, this author aims to ensure that no one gets left behind in the rapidly evolving world of crypto.

Table of Contents

Page 11

1. Introduction to Cryptocurrency

(1) - 1.1 What is Cryptocurrency?

(2) - 1.2 A Brief History of Crypto

(3) - 1.3 The Evolution of Digital Currency

Page 16

2. Understanding Blockchain Technology

(1) - 2.1 What is a Blockchain?

(2) - 2.2 How Blockchains Work

(3) - 2.3 Types of Blockchain Networks

3. The Value of Cryptocurrencies

(1) - 3.1 Factors Influencing Crypto Value

(2) - 3.2 Supply and Demand Dynamics

(3) - 3.3 The Role of Community and Use Cases

4. Different Types of Cryptocurrencies

(1) - 4.1 Bitcoin: The Pioneer

(2) - 4.2 Altcoins: Beyond Bitcoin

(3) - 4.3 Stablecoins: A Bridge to Stability

5. Getting Started with Investing in Crypto

(1) - 5.1 Choosing the Right Exchange

(2) - 5.2 Setting Up Your Wallet

(3) - 5.3 Understanding KYC and Security Measures

6. Crypto Trading Basics

(1) - 6.1 Types of Orders: Market vs Limit

(2) - 6.2 Reading Charts and Candlestick Patterns

(3) - 6.3 Essential Trading Terms to Know

7. Do's and Don'ts of Crypto Investing

(1) - 7.1 Common Mistakes to Avoid

(2) - 7.2 Best Practices for New Investors

(3) - 7.3 Diversification Strategies

8. Technical Analysis for New Traders

(1) - 8.1 Understanding Support and Resistance

(2) - 8.2 Key Indicators: RSI, MACD, and More

(3) - 8.3 Developing Your Own Trading Strategy

9. The Role of Regulation

(1) - 9.1 Government Approaches to Crypto

(2) - 9.2 The Impact of Regulations on Value

(3) - 9.3 Future Outlook on Crypto Regulation

10. The Future of Cryptocurrencies

(1) - 10.1 Emerging Trends and Technologies

(2) - 10.2 Predictions from Industry Experts

(3) - 10.3 How Crypto Could Transform Finance

11. Learning Resources for Crypto Enthusiasts

(1) - 11.1 Recommended Books and Articles

(2) - 11.2 Online Courses and Learning Platforms

(3) - 11.3 Communities and Networking Opportunities

12. The Psychological Aspect of Trading

(1) - 12.1 Understanding FOMO and FUD

(2) - 12.2 Managing Emotions in Trading

(3) - 12.3 Building Confidence as a New Investor

13. Case Studies in Crypto

(1) - 13.1 Success Stories: Big Wins in Crypto

(2) - 13.2 Lessons from Failed Projects

(3) - 13.3 Analyzing Market Patterns through History

14. Crypto in Everyday Life

(1) - 14.1 Merchants Accepting Cryptocurrency

(2) - 14.2 The Role of Crypto in Online Transactions

(3) - 14.3 Gaining Financial Independence with Crypto

15. Conclusion and Final Thoughts

(1) - 15.1 Recap of Key Takeaways

(2) - 15.2 Encouragement for New Investors

(3) - 15.3 The Importance of Continuous Learning

1. Introduction to Cryptocurrency

1.1 What is Cryptocurrency?

Cryptocurrency can be simply defined as a form of digital or virtual money that exists only online. It uses cryptography for security, making it difficult, if not impossible, to counterfeit or double-spend. This might sound technical, but at its core, cryptocurrency is just a new way to exchange value, like the cash you have in your wallet, but with the convenience of being entirely digital. As a new investor, you might find it helpful to think of it as a currency that operates without the need for physical coins or notes, and instead relies on a decentralized network called blockchain to manage transactions and keep everyone honest.

The beauty of cryptocurrencies lies in their independence from traditional banks. When you use a cryptocurrency, transactions happen directly between users, often with significantly lower fees compared to what you would pay at the bank or through a credit card. This peer-to-peer structure means that no one entity, like a big bank, has control over it. Instead, ownership and management are disbursed among a network of computers around the world. Each time you make a transaction, it gets recorded on the blockchain, a public ledger that everyone can see but none can easily alter. This transparency is reassuring, especially for those who may have lost faith in traditional banking systems.

Understanding cryptocurrencies opens up a new world of investment opportunities. So as you start your journey into the trading world, remember that the best part of it is getting to learn as you earn. Keep an eye on your charts and candlestick patterns, and don't hesitate to explore resources where you can deepen your knowledge, such as online forums or educational platforms. Stay curious, stay informed, and you might just find that this digital treasure map can lead you to some rewarding paths.

1.2 A Brief History of Crypto

Key milestones in the development of cryptocurrencies are fascinating and sometimes feel like a wild roller coaster ride that we've all been on. It all began in 2009 when Bitcoin was introduced by an unknown person or group using the name Satoshi Nakamoto. This innovative digital currency grabbed everyone's attention with its promise of decentralization and security. The underlying technology, blockchain, showcased how transactions could be recorded in a transparent, tamper-proof way. As time passed, Bitcoin paved the way for countless altcoins, each with its unique features and purposes, like Ethereum's smart contracts that revolutionized the world of decentralized applications. By 2013, Bitcoin reached significant milestones, like exceeding $1,000 in value, and it seemed like the entire universe had taken notice. However, it wasn't all smooth sailing. The Mt. Gox exchange scandal in 2014 showed how vulnerable this new world could be, with hackers making off with hundreds of thousands of bitcoins, putting investors on high alert.

Understanding how failures and successes have shaped the current crypto landscape proves to be just as essential as knowing its history. The boom of Initial Coin Offerings (ICOs) in 2017 was met with excitement, yet it also attracted scams and failures that left many without their hard-earned money. This roller coaster brought about greater regulatory scrutiny and the need for better protections for investors, particularly for newcomers trying to navigate these turbulent waters. Fast forward to 2021, when cryptocurrencies reached astronomical values, and institutional investors began to accept them, showcasing a notable shift in perception. Yet the journey is ongoing, with market fluctuations and regulatory changes continuously impacting investor sentiment. This lively world is filled with learning opportunities where both beginners and seasoned traders can analyze trends, run charts, and even dabble in candlestick readings to better understand market movements. A practical takeaway for anyone interested in crypto is to start small, educate yourself diligently, and always remain cautious. The crypto landscape is ever-evolving, and with the right knowledge, you just might catch the wave at the right moment.

1.3 The Evolution of Digital Currency

The journey of digital currency began long before Bitcoin made its grand entrance onto the world stage in 2009. Early forms of digital money emerged as innovative ideas, like e-gold, which allowed users to exchange gold electronically. This marked the first step toward a more decentralized financial model, pushing us away from traditional banking systems. It wasn't just about convenience; the desire for privacy and autonomy over one's own finances was the driving force behind these developments. With the rise of the internet, we began to witness a shift in how value could be transferred and perceived. Each advancement paved the way for newer concepts of currency, gradually leading to the birth of cryptocurrency, which offered an alternative that was not just digital but also decentralized. The introduction of blockchain technology was a significant breakthrough, creating a secure and transparent platform for transactions, enabling the notion of trust in a trustless environment.

Finding out how we got here would be incomplete without acknowledging the technological strides that propelled this evolution forward. From early encryption methods used for securing data to revolutionary inventions like peer-to-peer networking, each innovation has played a crucial role. The advent of smartphones and the widespread usage of the internet offered an accessible entry point for individuals to trade and invest. Moreover, developments in security technologies, like cryptographic algorithms, have reinforced the integrity of digital transactions, providing confidence to newer investors and traders. Companies that devised clever solutions to complex problems in transactions, wallets, and exchanges emerged, reshaping how we think about money. It's fascinating to see how a combination of technology and the human spirit for innovation has radically transformed our financial landscape. For those just stepping into this world, understanding these technological fundamentals will serve as a bedrock for your investment journey.

As you explore the world of digital currencies, remember that knowledge is your best ally. Take some time to familiarize yourself with the evolution of technology behind cryptocurrencies. It's not merely numbers on a screen; there's a rich history and an array of innovative ideas behind every digital coin. Equip yourself with reliable resources and stay updated on market dynamics. Learning how to read charts and understand candlestick patterns will set you apart, particularly in a volatile market. Don't hesitate to reach out and engage with communities online, where traders and investors share insights. Building your foundation now will pay off as you navigate this exciting and sometimes daunting landscape.

2. Understanding Blockchain Technology

2.1 What is a Blockchain?

Blockchain technology is like a digital ledger that records transactions or data in a way that makes it secure, transparent, and tamper-proof. Think of it as a collection of blocks, each containing information about transactions. Each block is linked to the previous one, forming a chain, which is where the name blockchain comes from. This technology serves as the backbone of cryptocurrencies, providing a means to verify transactions without needing a middleman, like a bank. It's a revolutionary step towards decentralization, which many find appealing because it puts control back in the hands of individuals rather than large institutions.

Understanding the core components of a blockchain is essential. Each block contains several key elements: a list of transactions, a timestamp, and a unique hash that identifies it. The hash also includes the hash of the previous block, creating an unbreakable link between them. This is what ensures the integrity of the whole structure—if someone tries to alter a block, its hash will change, and all subsequent hashes will become invalid. Decentralized networks support this technology, meaning there isn't a single point of failure. Instead, every participant in the network maintains a copy of the entire blockchain, which enhances security and transparency. It's like having a whole neighborhood looking after each house, ensuring that anything suspicious is quickly flagged, leaving no room for manipulation.

The beauty of blockchain comes from its potential and versatility. Beyond cryptocurrencies, many industries are exploring its use—from supply chain management to healthcare. As a new investor or trader, understanding this technology is vital as it underpins a vast number of digital assets. A practical tip to keep in mind is to always be cautious of projects claiming to use blockchain technology; not all implementations are created equal. Focus on those offering real solutions and don't get swayed by the hype. Being informed and questioning the validity and purpose of a blockchain project can be your best defense against falling for scams.

2.2 How Blockchains Work

Understanding blockchain transactions can feel like learning a new language, but once you break it down, it's surprisingly straightforward. When a transaction occurs, it begins with a request. Let's say you want to send some cryptocurrency to a friend. This request is then broadcast to a network of computers, also known as nodes, which are all keeping an eye on things. Each node receives this transaction and works to validate it. They check if you have enough cryptocurrency to complete the transaction and if it's not a double spend, which means trying to spend the same amount of currency twice. If everything checks out, the transaction moves to the next stage.

Once validated, your transaction is bundled together with others into a block. This block is then added to the existing chain of blocks – hence the term "blockchain." This is where the magic of consensus mechanisms comes into play. Consensus mechanisms are a set of protocols that nodes use to achieve agreement on the network about the state of the blockchain. One popular method is proof of work, where miners compete to solve complex mathematical puzzles. The first to solve it gets to add the block to the chain and earns a reward – kind of like winning a race where everyone else is still stuck in traffic! This process not only secures the network but also ensures that everyone has the same version of history, so to speak.

While all this might sound a bit technical, it is genuinely designed to foster trust and security in a decentralized manner. In the traditional banking world, a central authority validates transactions. In blockchain, that role is distributed across all nodes, which makes it incredibly hard for any malicious entity to change the past records without being detected. A useful tip to remember here is that the technology behind blockchain is still evolving, so staying curious and informed will significantly benefit you as you explore investment opportunities in this space.

2.3 Types of Blockchain Networks

Public, private, and consortium blockchains are the three major types of blockchain networks, and it's essential to understand the differences among them. Public blockchains are like the open highways of the internet. Anyone can join, participate, and view the transactions taking place. They are decentralized, meaning no single entity owns them. Think Bitcoin or Ethereum, where the focus is on transparency and inclusivity. On the other hand, private blockchains are more like exclusive clubs.

They require an invitation to join and typically are controlled by a single organization. This type of network is often utilized for internal business operations where privacy and speed are prioritized over full transparency. Consortium blockchains fall somewhere in between; imagine a group of friends who share a secret garden. Here, a few organizations work together, sharing control over the network while allowing certain levels of access to outside entities. These networks are often used in joint ventures between companies or in sectors like banking, where collaboration between parties can enhance trust while still maintaining some level of confidentiality.

Each type of blockchain comes with its unique use cases and advantages. Public blockchains shine when it comes to creating decentralized applications that benefit from a vast user base and high levels of trust—perfect for cryptocurrencies or any service requiring widespread adoption. Their transparency can foster confidence among users, making them ideal for fundraising or community-led projects. Private blockchains are like your traditional office network—very efficient for internal processes like supply chain management, where speed and confidentiality matter most. Organizations can customize these networks to suit their needs, optimizing performance and security without having to worry about external interference. Consortium blockchains benefit businesses that perform similar tasks and need a shared environment to collaborate without losing their distinct advantages. They can facilitate smoother operations in industries like healthcare and finance, where multiple players must work together while still guarding their sensitive data.

Understanding these distinctions empowers you as a new investor or trader. When you come across projects or companies utilizing blockchain, think about which type of network they are using and how it plays into their overall value proposition. This knowledge can significantly enhance your decision-making process. Remember, whether you're a boomer or a Gen Xer diving into this space for the first time, educating yourself on how these different blockchains function will ultimately give you an edge. A practical tip? Look for projects that operate on consortium blockchains if you value collaborative endeavors—it often leads to significant advancements in technology and efficiency while also fostering trust among organizations.

3. The Value of Cryptocurrencies

3.1 Factors Influencing Crypto Value

Market sentiment plays a monumental role in the world of cryptocurrency. Unlike traditional stocks, which have certain fundamentals that can be analyzed, cryptocurrencies often thrive or dive based on the emotional pulse of their investors. A single tweet from a prominent figure or a sensational news headline can send prices spiraling or soaring within hours. During my time in trading, I've witnessed how panic during market dips can cause people to sell and subsequently lose out on potential gains. On the flip side, exuberance can drive an asset to the moon, often on thin air. Events like regulatory announcements, technological breakthroughs, or even celebrity endorsements can create a frenzied atmosphere, leading traders to act swiftly, sometimes without considering the underlying value of what they're trading. Remember, staying informed and analyzing the bigger picture amidst all the noise can help guide your decisions.

Technological innovation is the bedrock of cryptocurrency, but speculation often stirs the pot. As much as we all love the idea of a blockchain revolution, much of the investment in cryptocurrencies hinges on perceptions of value rather than the technology itself. I've had moments where I've invested in a coin simply because it sounded revolutionary, only to later realize that the project was still in its infancy, without any real-world application. It's essential to strike a balance between recognizing genuine technological advancements—like enhanced security features, scalability solutions, or groundbreaking applications—and the aura of intrigue that speculation brings. A sound approach involves digging deep: examining the creators, understanding their vision, reading whitepapers, and checking community feedback to avoid getting swept away by hype. Consider every investment carefully, like you're curating a fine collection, rather than haphazardly tossing coins into a wishing well.

Pay attention to the ever-shifting landscape of cryptocurrency. Resources like online forums, webinars, and educational content can be a goldmine for new investors and traders. Having a solid grasp of technical analysis, including charts and candlestick readings, can provide you with insights you might not get from just following the news. Combining the emotional understanding of market sentiment with the analytical skills of tech-driven assessment can empower your trading journey, leading to better decisions in a volatile market.

3.2 Supply and Demand Dynamics

Understanding the basic economic principles of supply and demand is crucial, especially in the context of cryptocurrency. At its core, supply refers to how much of a particular asset is available for purchase, while demand reflects how much people want that asset. In the world of crypto, this relationship can shift dramatically due to various factors, such as market sentiment, technological advancements, and regulatory news. For instance, a sudden increase in interest from institutional investors can ramp up demand for a cryptocurrency, pushing its price to new heights. Conversely, if there's news of a hack or regulatory crackdown, the demand can plummet, resulting in a rapid decline in value. Being aware of these dynamics allows investors and traders to make informed decisions and anticipate potential market movements.

Limited supply is one of the most fascinating aspects when it comes to certain cryptocurrencies, particularly Bitcoin. Bitcoin's supply is capped at 21 million coins, and this scarcity can lead to increased value over time. As more people get interested in Bitcoin, and the supply remains fixed, the classic law of supply and demand kicks in—the highly sought-after asset gains value simply because there are fewer of them available. This principle also applies to other cryptocurrencies as they introduce mechanisms such as burning tokens or having a max supply. As new investors, it's essential to recognize how a currency's supply limitations can drive its price upward, especially when accompanied by strong demand or positive market trends. By keeping an eye on these factors, anyone can gain a better understanding of how to navigate the crypto landscape more effectively.

When getting started with trading or investing in cryptocurrencies, one practical tip is to regularly check the market cap and circulating supply of a cryptocurrency. These numbers provide valuable insights into its relative worth and potential for growth. As you explore the world of crypto, remember that it's not just about what you buy but also about understanding why it matters. Knowing how supply and demand affect your assets gives you an edge, helping you avoid common pitfalls and pick potential winners.

3.3 The Role of Community and Use Cases

The importance of community engagement and active user bases in boosting a crypto's value cannot be overstated. Imagine a bustling marketplace filled with traders and enthusiasts eager to discuss and promote their favorite cryptocurrencies. This vibrant environment not only creates buzz but also fosters trust and credibility. When people feel connected to a community, they're more likely to invest, trade, and advocate for the currency, creating a cycle of growth and support. The power of word-of-mouth within these communities should never be underestimated. As newcomers, engaging with these groups opens doors to insights and resources that can prove invaluable in the tumultuous world of crypto.

Examining real-world applications reveals just how certain cryptocurrencies lend credibility and utility. Take, for instance, Bitcoin, which has established itself as a digital gold. It's not just a speculative asset; it's being used for transactions and as a store of value in countries facing economic instability. Then there are cryptocurrencies like Ethereum, which power decentralized applications and smart contracts, making them essential in the tech landscape. These practical uses breed confidence in potential investors and users. Real-world applications help bridge the gap between digital currencies and everyday life, showing us that crypto isn't just a trend but a fundamental shift in how we consider value and transactions.

A practical tip for new investors is to not only look at the price movements on charts but also to engage actively with the community behind a currency. Follow forums, join social media groups, and participate in discussions. By understanding the use cases and the community's perspective, you can make more informed decisions about where to invest your hard-earned money. Remember, a strong community can often signal a promising future for a cryptocurrency, while practical applications can solidify its place in the financial landscape.

4. Different Types of Cryptocurrencies

4.1 Bitcoin: The Pioneer

Bitcoin stands as the first cryptocurrency, breaking barriers and paving the way for the digital currency revolution. Launched in 2009 by an unknown person or group of people using the pseudonym Satoshi Nakamoto, Bitcoin was created as a response to the flaws in our traditional banking systems, offering a decentralized financial model that allows peer-to-peer transactions without the need for intermediaries. Its success in capturing the imagination of both tech enthusiasts and investors has solidified its position as the leading cryptocurrency, the benchmark by which all others are measured. As a new investor, it's fascinating to see how Bitcoin has not only maintained its dominance in the market but has also become synonymous with the concept of cryptocurrency itself. This is where things get a bit interesting—Bitcoin is not just a financial asset; it's a cultural phenomenon, creating communities and driving innovations like nothing we've seen before.

What really sets Bitcoin apart from the sea of other cryptocurrencies is its unique features. Firstly, there's the fundamental aspect of scarcity. Bitcoin's supply is capped at 21 million coins, making it inherently limited, akin to precious metals like gold. This scarcity creates demand and, alongside a growing acceptance of Bitcoin in various markets and platforms, helps to maintain its value. Additionally, the underlying technology, blockchain, is a marvel in itself. It's an immutable ledger that ensures transactions are recorded transparently and securely, providing a level of trust and accountability that traditional banking has often struggled to achieve. Unlike many altcoins that might seem to pop up like mushrooms after rain, Bitcoin's security is bolstered by a massive network of miners who validate and confirm transactions. This has built a resilient infrastructure that, despite its volatility in price, holds a significant part of both public trust and investor interest. For the new trader or investor, understanding these distinct qualities can be the key to navigating the complexities of the crypto market.

4.2 Altcoins: Beyond Bitcoin

Altcoins, or alternative coins to Bitcoin, have gained significant traction in the ever-evolving cryptocurrency landscape. While Bitcoin often steals the limelight as the pioneering cryptocurrency, altcoins serve as a flourishing ecosystem that broadens the possibilities of blockchain technology. These coins have emerged for various reasons, like improving transaction speeds, offering unique features, or focusing on specific industries. Their rise reflects an innovation spirit, catering to differing needs and preferences in finance and technology.

Among the noteworthy altcoins, Ethereum stands tall. Not just a digital currency, it brings smart contracts into play, allowing developers to create decentralized applications. Then there's Ripple, which aims to revolutionize cross-border payments, demonstrating how blockchain can streamline financial transactions globally. Another compelling example is Chainlink, which connects smart contracts with real-world data, enhancing their utility. Each of these altcoins showcases specific use cases that address unique challenges, proving that there's a world of options beyond Bitcoin, each brimming with potential.

As you delve into the realm of altcoins, it's vital to research and understand their specific use cases before investing. Each altcoin comes with its own story, values, and technology. Don't be swayed solely by trends; engage with communities, read up on whitepapers, and familiarize yourself with the project's goals. This knowledge will not only aid in making informed investment decisions but also enhance your appreciation for this dynamic crypto universe.

4.3 Stablecoins: A Bridge to Stability

Stablecoins are innovative digital currencies designed to maintain a stable value by pegging them to a reserve of assets, such as fiat currency or commodities. This concept addresses one of the primary obstacles in the volatile world of cryptocurrencies. Unlike Bitcoin or Ethereum, whose prices can swing wildly in a matter of hours, stablecoins like USDC or Tether offer a more predictable experience. For new investors and traders, this stability can be a breath of fresh air, especially during turbulent market conditions. It allows you to engage with the cryptocurrency space without the constant worry of a rollercoaster ride on your investment. By utilizing stablecoins, you can sidestep much of the chaos while still participating in trading, transfers, and other dynamics of the market.

There are generally three main types of stablecoins: fiat-collateralized, crypto-collateralized, and algorithmic stablecoins. Each type plays a unique role in the ecosystem. Fiat-collateralized stablecoins, such as Tether (USDT) and USD Coin (USDC), are backed 1:1 by traditional currencies like the US dollar. This relationship makes them a popular choice for everyday transactions and trading pairs on exchanges, providing a seamless bridge between the worlds of fiat and crypto. On the other hand, crypto-collateralized stablecoins, like DAI, use other cryptocurrencies as collateral, which adds a layer of complexity. Finally, algorithmic stablecoins use algorithms and smart contracts to control supply and demand, aiming to maintain their stable value without being directly backed by reserves. Each type of stablecoin offers different advantages and may appeal to various types of users, whether they are seasoned traders or newcomers dipping their toes into the water.

Understanding how to use stablecoins effectively can position you for success in your trading adventures. If you find yourself navigating a volatile market, consider keeping a portion of your portfolio in stablecoins. This strategy not only allows you to take advantage of price drops but also provides a safe haven for your gains. Think of stablecoins as a financial life raft; when the waves get too rough, you can hop on and wait for calmer seas. Always remember, whether you're a boomer who loves the safety of predictability or a GenXer exploring new opportunities, stablecoins offer a balance of innovation and stability that can enhance your crypto experience.

5. Getting Started with Investing in Crypto

5.1 Choosing the Right Exchange

When diving into the world of cryptocurrency, picking the right exchange can feel like trying to decipher a complex puzzle. There are several factors that come into play. First and foremost, you need to consider the fees. Some exchanges offer low trading fees, which can be appealing, especially if you plan to trade frequently. However, remember to look out for withdrawal fees and deposit fees, as these can add up quickly and eat into your profits.

Next, security features are a must-have consideration. The last thing you want is to wake up one day to find your crypto assets have disappeared. Verify if the exchange has insurance policies in place or utilizes cold storage for the majority of its assets. User reviews can provide insights into the experiences of others regarding the security of the platform, so do your homework before settling on an exchange.

Now, let's take a closer look at some popular exchanges. Coinbase is often the first stop for many new investors due to its user-friendly interface. It's like the kindergarten of cryptocurrency—simple and accessible, but some might find its fees on the higher side for frequent trading. Binance, on the other hand, offers a huge variety of cryptocurrencies with lower fees, making it a great choice for those looking to explore beyond the mainstream options. While it has a steeper learning curve, once you get the hang of it, it opens up a world of possibilities.

Then you have Kraken, which is well-regarded for its robust security features and advanced trading options. It's the exchange for those who want to dive deeper into the cryptocurrency seas and are ready to tackle a bit more complexity. For students and new investors, this might seem daunting but fear not; most exchanges offer educational resources to help you navigate the waters. Lastly, consider platforms like Gemini and eToro, which have their unique offerings, such as social trading features that can be particularly helpful for beginners wanting to learn from more experienced traders.

When choosing an exchange, think about not just what you need now, but also what you might need in the future. If you're a new trader, it can be beneficial to opt for platforms that offer educational materials or community support. Jumping in with both feet can be thrilling, so stay informed, keep your expectations in check, and don't hesitate to reach out for help if you feel overwhelmed. And hey, when in doubt, always double-check your selections and ensure you're investing in a way that feels comfortable for you.

5.2 Setting Up Your Wallet

When diving into the world of cryptocurrency, understanding the various types of wallets is crucial. Hot wallets are those that are connected to the internet, making them convenient for quick transactions, but they are also more susceptible to hacking. Cold wallets, on the other hand, are not connected to the internet, offering better security for long-term storage of your digital assets. Then there are hardware wallets, which are a form of cold wallet but come in the shape of a physical device. Choosing the best wallet depends on what you plan to do with your investment; if you're looking to trade frequently, a hot wallet might serve you well, whereas for holding a large amount of cryptocurrency securely, a cold wallet or hardware wallet is advisable. A little research goes a long way in finding the right option for your specific needs.

Now that you know about the types of wallets, let's get down to the nitty-gritty of setting one up. Start by selecting the wallet type that suits your needs. If you've opted for a hot wallet, visit the website of the wallet provider and download the application. Make sure it's legitimate—don't fall for scams! After installation, the app will guide you through the process of creating your wallet. You will typically need to set up a strong password and back up your recovery phrase, which is crucial for recovering your wallet if you forget your password. This is the time to get a bit paranoid! Write it down and keep it in a safe place. For hardware wallets, the setup process usually involves connecting the device to your computer, following the instructions that come with it, and making sure to initialize it with a secure PIN code. When you're done, test your wallet with a smaller amount to ensure everything works, before trusting it with your larger investments. Always remember: security is your best friend in this digital landscape.

Consider this handy tip: enable two-factor authentication (2FA) no matter which wallet you choose. This adds an extra layer of security that can save you from a world of headaches later on. Cryptocurrency is an exciting investment opportunity, but it comes with its own set of risks. Keeping your investments secure should be your top priority as you embark on your trading journey.

5.3 Understanding KYC and Security Measures

Know Your Customer (KYC) regulations are essential tools aimed at preventing fraud and money laundering in the world of cryptocurrencies. For new investors and traders, understanding these regulations is crucial because they help establish trust in a market that can sometimes feel chaotic and risky. KYC involves verifying the identity of customers and ensuring that they are who they say they are. It's like getting to know a new neighbor before borrowing a cup of sugar; you want to make sure they're reliable and not just a figment of the street corner. By complying with KYC, exchanges can create a safer trading environment, which is something we all want, right? Moreover, for people venturing into crypto, adhering to these regulations can also mean avoiding potential legal headaches down the road. Compliance helps to legitimize the market and protects you from being unknowingly involved in illicit activities. So, before diving headlong into trading, take a moment to understand your chosen platform's KYC practices. It may seem like a hassle, but it's a protective barrier against some of the wild stuff that can happen in the crypto space.

Securing your investments in the crypto world is like putting on a seatbelt before a drive—you hope you won't need it, but it's better to be safe than sorry. Start with choosing a strong password and enable two-factor authentication wherever possible. This adds an extra layer of security and can thwart hackers who might try to access your account. I once heard of a trader who had his Bitcoin stolen because he used a simple password; a painful lesson that was unfortunately all too common. Additionally, be cautious about sharing your information online. Scammers often use social engineering tactics to trick individuals into revealing sensitive information. If something feels off, trust your gut! It's wise to store your cryptocurrencies in hardware wallets instead of keeping them on exchanges. Think of hardware wallets as a safe where you can store valuable items; it's a physical device that protects your assets offline. Always keep your software up to date, use antivirus programs, and keep an eye out for any phishing emails that might come your way. The internet can be a wild place, and staying vigilant will help you dodge many pitfalls.

As you navigate through the exciting world of cryptocurrency investing, remember that security and compliance are your best friends. Take the time to educate yourself, invest in proper tools, and implement the necessary safeguards. There's nothing funny about losing your hard-earned funds to scams or hacks. Engage with trusted communities and always strive to stay informed about the latest threats and protective measures. This journey is as much about learning as it is about profit, so keep that spirit alive! Having this knowledge not only prepares you for a smoother ride but can also turn the tumultuous waves of crypto trading into a more manageable experience.

6. Crypto Trading Basics

6.1 Types of Orders: Market vs Limit

Understanding the fundamental difference between market and limit orders is vital for anyone stepping into the world of trading. A market order is a type of order to buy or sell a stock immediately at the best available current price. This means that if you place a market order, you might purchase a stock for slightly more or get a little less than you expected, depending on market fluctuations at that moment. It's perfect for those situations when speed is essential, such as if there's a piece of breaking news you want to act upon quickly. On the other hand, a limit order sets a specific price at which you are willing to buy or sell a stock. This gives you the flexibility to only transact on favorable terms, but of course, there's a trade-off: if the stock doesn't reach that price, your order won't be executed. The trick is knowing when to use which type. Market orders are great for trades you want to execute immediately, while limit orders work well when you have a specific price target in mind and can afford to wait a bit longer for it.

To illustrate these concepts, let's say you're interested in a stock currently trading at $50. If you think it will rise quickly because of new product news and want to get in right away, placing a market order could be your best bet. You might end up buying it for $50.25, but you secured your position before the price shoots up. Now, imagine a different scenario: You believe that the stock's true value is closer to $48, and you're willing to wait it out. In this case, you would set a limit order to buy at $48. If the market swings down to that price, your order will execute, but if it doesn't, that money stays in your pocket, waiting for the right opportunity. Each option has its strengths and realizing when to pull the trigger on either one can really work to your advantage.

Investing is about making informed choices. When first starting out, remember that using market orders can feel like a safe way to dive in, but don't just jump in without a plan. Combine your understanding of market and limit orders with proper research on stock fundamentals, charts, and candlestick patterns. This balanced approach will help you make smarter decisions as you navigate the waves of the stock market.

6.2 Reading Charts and Candlestick Patterns

Crypto charts are like the pulse of the market, giving us vital signs on how cryptocurrencies are performing. Understanding these charts is crucial for anyone diving into the world of trading. You can't just jump in and hope for the best; you need to read the data, and that's where candlestick patterns come into play. Each candlestick represents a specific time frame, showing the open, high, low, and close prices of a cryptocurrency. When you start piecing together these patterns, you gain insight into the market's mood. Are investors feeling bullish, or is a bear lurking around the corner? The configuration of these candles can signal potential buying or selling opportunities, making them a trader's best friend. Just remember, though, these patterns are as much about psychology as they are about numbers. When you see a specific formation, think about what it implies for investor sentiment. Developing this intuition can take time, but it's an essential part of your trading journey.

The journey of reading charts and candlestick patterns is ongoing, and even seasoned traders still learn every day. I find it helpful to continually educate myself. There are some fantastic resources out there, from online courses to forums and books that delve deeply into technical analysis. Look for communities where you can ask questions and share insights—sometimes, a conversation with a fellow trader can spark a new understanding. Remember, producing consistent results takes both study and practice. Consider paper trading to test your newfound skills without risking your hard-earned money. Set aside time each week just for analysis; make it a habit. Over time, as you decipher these patterns like a seasoned detective, you'll not only feel more confident but also more equipped to navigate this fascinating world of crypto trading.

6.3 Essential Trading Terms to Know

Understanding essential trading terms is like learning to read the map before embarking on a journey. Terms like order books, liquidity, and market capitalization (market cap) form the backbone of trading knowledge. An order book is essentially a list of buy and sell orders for a particular asset, showing what people are willing to pay and accept. It's like a community bulletin board where everyone can see what's available and when deals are happening. Liquidity, on the other hand, represents how easily you can buy or sell an asset without causing a significant impact on its price. Think of it as the difference between selling a hot cupcake at a crowded fair versus a dusty old cookie in an empty pantry; one is much easier to unload than the other! Market cap is another crucial term, as it indicates the total value of all a company's shares, calculated by multiplying the stock price by the total number of outstanding shares. This figure helps investors determine the size of a company and its place in the market hierarchy, allowing for more informed decision-making.

On your journey as a new trader, being fluent in these crucial terms is essential for navigating the often-tumultuous trading environment with confidence. It's kind of like learning the lingo in a foreign country; the more phrases and terms you know, the easier it will be to engage with the locals—in this case, the market. Knowing when and how to use terms like "bull market" (where prices are rising) versus "bear market" (where prices are falling) will help you make educated trades and better understand market sentiments. Additionally, grasping concepts like support and resistance can empower you to take more calculated risks. Support levels indicate where prices tend to stop falling and may bounce back up, while resistance levels indicate price points where trends may reverse. Becoming familiar with these terms will not only enhance your comprehension but also increase your comfort level during your trading strategy discussions.

When diving into the trading world, it's vital to keep a toolkit of resources at hand. Books, educational websites, and even trading apps can help boost your knowledge. Joining forums or groups where traders share best practices can also be incredibly helpful. Remember that everyone, even the seasoned pros, started just where you are now. Learning the lingo and concepts of trading takes time and patience. Take it slow, incorporate what you learn step by step, and don't hesitate to ask questions. If you feel lost, just know that every trader has felt that way. The key is to keep looking for the information that resonates with you and aligns with your trading goals. Keeping your mindset adaptable will surely lead you to become a proficient trader.

7. Do's and Don'ts of Crypto Investing

7.1 Common Mistakes to Avoid

Many novice investors trip over the same common pitfalls, often out of sheer excitement or lack of experience. One major mistake is chasing trends, investing in stocks that are currently popular without doing adequate research. It's like jumping on a train that's flying down the tracks with no guarantee where it will stop. Instead, grounding your decisions in solid research and a clear understanding of your own financial goals is vital. Another frequent error is overtrading. The allure of quick profits can blind you to the dangers of constantly buying and selling. Just because you can make a trade doesn't mean you should. Keeping a balanced approach and knowing when to stand still can save you a lot of time and stress. Emotional investing is another trap; letting fear or greed dictate your decisions can lead to rash actions and, before you know it, your portfolio is taking a nosedive.

Let me share a story about an eager newbie I know, whom I'll call Tom. Tom was pumped about investing in technology stocks after hearing friends rave about the latest hot company. He jumped in without researching how the company's financials aligned with its stock price. A month later, he watched in horror as the stock plummeted. Instead of losing faith, Tom turned to education, diving into books and resources that taught him how to analyze stocks properly. His experience illustrates that we all make mistakes; it's our ability to learn from them that truly matters. Another friend, Sarah, was so focused on daily price movements that she hardly slept at night, worrying about her investments. Eventually, she realized she was burning herself out. By setting a rule to only check her portfolio once a week, her stress levels decreased dramatically, and she could focus on her long-term strategies without losing sleep.

These experiences highlight that every misstep can serve as a lesson, reinforcing the idea that investing is a journey and not just a quest for quick gains. Embrace the learning process while maintaining an informed approach to investing. Remember, it's okay to start small, work on understanding the dynamics of the market, and use dependable resources for guidance. The key is to frame your investing not just as a way to make money, but as a learning opportunity. Always be willing to step back, reassess your strategies, and know that even seasoned investors continue to learn with each twist and turn in the market.

7.2 Best Practices for New Investors

Building a disciplined investment approach is key to success and keeping your cool during market fluctuations is crucial. Reacting impulsively to market movements can derail your plans faster than you can say market crash. It's natural to feel the adrenaline rush when stocks surge or plummet, but training yourself to pause and reflect is essential. Slow down, breathe, and assess the situation. Ask yourself if your decision aligns with your long-term goals. Creating a well-thought-out investment strategy, one that is clearly defined and rooted in your personal financial objectives, can help you resist the urge to make rash decisions. It's like having a trusted GPS guiding you on a road trip—no matter how tempting it is to take a shortcut when you see a detour, staying on your planned route will lead to a better outcome.

Research is the backbone of successful investing. Staying informed about the market and understanding what drives price movements can empower your decision-making process. Whether it's analyzing company earnings reports, scrutinizing economic indicators, or simply keeping an eye on market trends, knowledge is your friend. In this information age, a wealth of resources is at your fingertips—books, podcasts, financial news websites, and even social media forums like Twitter and Reddit can offer insights. Connecting with seasoned investors or enrolling in educational courses can deepen your understanding of charts, candlestick patterns, and overall market behavior. It's like equipping yourself with a treasure map; the more you know, the more confident you'll feel about your investment decisions.

A practical tip to keep in mind is to create a dedicated schedule for your research and analysis. Set aside specific times each week to update yourself on market trends and review your portfolio. This structured approach not only keeps you informed but also establishes consistency in your investment routine. Just like regular exercise is essential for physical health, regular market research is vital for your financial well-being. Embrace the journey of learning and remember, it's not just about where you invest but how informed and prepared you are along the way.

7.3 Diversification Strategies

Diversifying investments is crucial for anyone looking to decrease risk and enhance potential rewards. Think of it like having a safety net under a tightrope. If you only walk one rope—say, tech stocks—and that rope frays, a fall could be catastrophic. By spreading your investments across various assets, you cushion any blows from market volatility. This strategy allows you to capture gains from different sectors rather than holding all your eggs in one fragile basket. When the market behaves unpredictably, as it often does, a well-diversified portfolio can help to stabilize your returns and provide some peace of mind.

Now, let's dive into the fascinating world of cryptocurrency. Diversifying a crypto portfolio can be a bit like exploring a new and exciting restaurant menu. Instead of just ordering the same dish repeatedly, why not sample a variety of flavors? One effective way is to invest in a mix of well-established cryptocurrencies, like Bitcoin and Ethereum, along with some promising altcoins. But be mindful; not all altcoins are created equal. It's important to do your homework, researching projects that have solid use cases and active development teams. Additionally, consider diversifying into different blockchain sectors—such as DeFi projects, NFTs, or blockchain gaming. This way, when one area shines, it may compensate for underperforming assets in another.

Remember, the goal of diversification isn't just spreading investments around; it's about understanding how different assets interact with one another. Sometimes, a little humor can ease the stress of market movements. Think of your investments like a family reunion: some relatives might annoy you, but you tolerate them because they balance out the family dynamics! In crypto, however, it's crucial to keep a close eye on trends and market sentiment. Regularly revisiting your portfolio and adjusting based on changing landscapes can help you maximize your chances for growth. A good tip here is to look for projects that are resilient during market downturns—they're like your wise old uncle at the reunion, always offering sage advice! Keep learning, stay curious, and your diversified investments will likely serve you well.

8. Technical Analysis for New Traders

8.1 Understanding Support and Resistance

Support and resistance levels are fundamental concepts in the world of trading, and they can significantly influence price movements in the market. Support refers to a price level where a stock or asset tends to stop falling and may even bounce back upward, acting almost like a safety net. It's as if the stock finds a comfortable floor, making it hard for the price to drop further. Resistance, on the other hand, is the ceiling where the price seems to struggle to rise above. Picture a stubborn teenager trying to jump higher, but there's an invisible ceiling that keeps bringing them back down. Recognizing these levels can be critical because they help traders make informed decisions about when to buy or sell. Understanding where these levels are located is like having a map in a new city; it prevents you from taking unnecessary detours that could lead to losses.

Identifying support and resistance on trading charts might sound a bit daunting at first, but it's a skill that can be developed with practice and a little patience. Look closely at historical price movements; areas where the price has repeatedly bounced back up are often support levels, while areas where the price has struggled to break through usually indicate resistance. You can draw horizontal lines at these key levels to create a visual representation on your charts. Candlestick patterns often reveal more about these levels too. For instance, when you notice a strong reversal candlestick pattern forming at a support level, it might signal a potential buying opportunity. Perhaps you have a friend who loves to share memes; finding these levels is a similar adventure—looking for those funny moments where everything aligns perfectly!

As you venture into this fascinating world of support and resistance, remember, patience is your ally. Analyze the charts, give yourself time to absorb the patterns, and don't hesitate to use trading simulators to practice without financial risk. The more you familiarize yourself with these concepts, the more adept you will become at identifying potential entry and exit points. A practical tip is to always use multiple time frames when identifying these levels, as what may seem like resistance on a daily chart could act as support on a weekly chart. By being aware of this, you can align your trading strategies with the broader market trends, ensuring a smoother and more informed trading experience.

8.2 Key Indicators: RSI, MACD, and More

Key technical indicators are essential for traders who want to understand market trends and make informed investment decisions. Two of the most widely used indicators are the Relative Strength Index (RSI) and the Moving Average Convergence Divergence (MACD). The RSI measures the speed and change of price movements, giving you insights into whether a stock is overbought or oversold. This can be particularly helpful when you're trying to decide if it's time to jump in or sit back for a while. On the other hand, the MACD is a trend-following momentum indicator that shows the relationship between two moving averages of a security's price. It's fantastic for spotting changes in the strength, direction, momentum, and duration of a trend in a stock's price. Along with these, there are other tools you can use, but starting with these two will set a solid foundation.

Using technical indicators like RSI and MACD in your decision-making process can be a game changer. For instance, a high RSI, typically above 70, suggests that a stock might be overbought and due for a price correction, making it a potential time to sell or avoid buying. Conversely, an RSI below 30 indicates oversold conditions, signaling a potential buying opportunity. With MACD, looking for crossover points between the MACD line and the signal line can help you identify potential buy or sell signals. When the MACD line crosses above the signal line, it's often taken as a bullish signal, while crossing below indicates a bearish signal. The key is to interpret these indicators alongside other factors like market news and overall sentiment. It's not just about following numbers—it's about understanding what they imply for the market.

As you explore these tools, keep in mind that no indicator is perfect. It's vital to combine insights from various indicators with your personal research. Over-relying on just a single indicator can lead you astray, but when used wisely, RSI and MACD can greatly enhance your trading strategy. They can help you avoid common mistakes new investors often make, like chasing after a stock that's already peaked. So, take the time to practice using these indicators on charts and candlesticks while noting how they perform in different market conditions. This hands-on experience will build your confidence as a trader. Additionally, books and online resources about technical analysis can offer valuable guidance—they're worth diving into as they can make the learning journey more enjoyable and enlightening.

8.3 Developing Your Own Trading Strategy

```html
Crafting a personalized trading strategy is an essential step for new traders, and it should be based on individual goals and risk tolerance. Think of your goals as the North Star guiding your trading journey. Are you looking for steady income, or is your aim to build long-term wealth? Understanding whether you lean more towards a conservative or aggressive approach is crucial. Risk tolerance can be boiled down to figuring out how much loss you can stomach without losing your mind. Some traders feel comfortable with large swings in their portfolio, while others might get jittery at the first hint of loss. Establishing this baseline will help shape your trading decisions.

Just remember that developing a trading strategy is not a one-and-done deal. It's more of an ongoing journey than a destination. The markets are ever-changing, and so should your approach. The best traders regularly look back at their trades and analyze what worked and what didn't. This process of reflection and adjustment is what we call refining your approach. It's perfectly normal to tweak your strategies over time as you gain experience and grow more adept at reading those charts
```

and candlesticks. Everyone starts somewhere, and with each trade, you'll gain insights that can lead to enhancements in your strategy.

As you embark on this process, equip yourself with the right resources. There are countless books, webinars, and online communities where experienced traders share their wisdom. Engaging with these resources can offer new perspectives and make a substantial difference in your growth. One practical tip? Keep a trading journal. Documenting your trades, the reasons behind your decisions, and the outcomes can be immensely beneficial. Over time, you'll begin to see patterns in your trading habits that can inform future strategies. Embrace the journey—it's all part of becoming a savvy trader.

9. The Role of Regulation

9.1 Government Approaches to Crypto

Different countries are taking unique paths regarding the regulation of cryptocurrencies. In some places, governments are embracing digital currencies, aiming to harness innovation and ensure consumer protection. Countries like Portugal and Germany have adopted relatively friendly stances, often offering clear guidelines that encourage trading while minimizing the regulatory burden. In contrast, nations like China have declared outright bans, citing concerns over financial stability and illicit activities. This divergence in approach can create a regulatory mosaic that leaves investors scratching their heads and wondering where to safely plant their trading roots.

Comparing lenient and strict regulatory frameworks reveals notable impacts on cryptocurrency marketplaces. Countries with relaxed regulations often see vibrant trading communities springing up, fueled by innovation and an entrepreneurial spirit. In these environments, startups can flourish, and the overall market can benefit from active participation. However, lax regulations can also lead to issues like scams and uncertainty, causing many potential investors to hesitate. On the other hand, strict regulations can provide a sense of security and legitimacy, which may attract more mainstream financial players. Yet, they can also stifle innovation and drive traders to offshore markets, reducing local business opportunities. Finding that balance is pivotal, and each nation's choice impacts how cryptocurrencies evolve on their turf.

The landscape is dynamic, requiring investors to stay informed about the regulatory environment of their chosen investments. A reminder: before diving into trading, make sure you're aware of the regulations in your country. This knowledge can not only protect your investment but also guide your trading strategies moving forward.

9.2 The Impact of Regulations on Value

Regulatory news can swing prices in the cryptocurrency market like a pendulum on a wild ride. One announcement can send prices soaring, while another might have investors scrambling for the exits. For example, when governments around the world announce new regulations or policies regarding cryptocurrency trading or usage, it often creates immediate and noticeable effects on the market's value. Investors may react to news of stricter regulations by selling off their assets, fearing that compliance costs or restrictive measures could cut into profits. On the flip side, positive news, such as a government endorsing cryptocurrency or creating favorable regulations, can lead to a surge in purchases and investments, driving prices higher. It's like a game of emotional chess, where each new regulatory move can alter the entire board. Understanding this relationship between regulations and market fluctuations is essential for new investors and traders navigating this volatile landscape.

Real-world examples are abundant, as we can look at instances such as China's crackdown on cryptocurrency mining and trading in 2021. This news sent shockwaves through the market, resulting in Bitcoin's price plummeting significantly. Conversely, when El Salvador made headlines by adopting Bitcoin as legal tender, the markets reacted positively, showing how favorable legislation can boost confidence and value. Another notable case was when the U.S. Senate proposed a series of regulations aimed at protecting investors while clarifying the legal status of cryptocurrencies. Despite some initial skepticism, the long-term outlook from those regulations helped stabilize investor confidence, demonstrating that well-structured regulation can play a role in fostering a healthy market. These examples underline how sensitive the cryptocurrency market is to government influences, reminding us that staying updated on regulatory developments is crucial for those managing investments in this space.

For anyone venturing into cryptocurrency trading, it's vital to keep an ear to the ground regarding regulatory news. Utilizing resources such as government websites, reliable news outlets, and cryptocurrency forums can help you stay informed. Being proactive about understanding how regulations might impact your investments will not only help you react swiftly but also allow you to strategize thoughtfully. Remember, markets often reflect not just current realities but also investor sentiment and potential future developments. A little foresight can go a long way in making informed investment decisions.

9.3 Future Outlook on Crypto Regulation

Many of us find ourselves pondering the future of cryptocurrency regulations as the market continues to evolve at lightning speed. It's almost like trying to predict the weather in a hurricane; one day it's sunny, and the next, there's a storm brewing. Speculation about regulations has been rife among investors and enthusiasts alike. Over the next few years, we might see a patchwork of regulations emerge across different jurisdictions, which could either encourage healthy competition or create confusing barriers. Countries such as the United States and those in the European Union are likely to take the lead in shaping these rules, driven by a mix of political, economic, and social pressures. There's a strong likelihood that regulations will focus on areas such as anti-money laundering (AML) laws and know-your-customer (KYC) compliance, all in an effort to make the space safer for regular folks just trying to invest their hard-earned cash. And wouldn't that be a welcome change? By ensuring heightened security and transparency, we can create an environment that fosters trust. At the end of the day, I hope for a scenario where clarity in the rules leads people to feel empowered rather than restricted when they navigate the crypto realm.

Balancing innovation and consumer protection is a tightrope that governments must walk carefully. On one hand, they need to nurture the entrepreneurial spirit that cryptocurrencies ignite, allowing businesses to innovate without being stifled by overly restrictive measures. On the other hand, with the rapid rise of scams and shady practices in the crypto world, regulators also have the heavy responsibility to safeguard consumers from falling into traps. New investors, whether from the boomer or GenX generations, often dive into crypto without fully understanding the risks involved. It's heartbreaking to witness the disillusionment when they encounter fraud or lose money due to bad investments. So, it's clear that the government's aim will be to strike a balance, promoting a favorable environment for cryptocurrency growth while simultaneously ensuring that the vibrant and sometimes chaotic market doesn't turn into a free-for-all, with unsuspecting investors left holding the bag.

Future regulations will likely redefine the landscape of crypto trading as we know it today. Investors should stay informed and adaptable, as knowledge is your best defense. Understanding the potential regulations can provide insight into market sentiment and help navigate the inevitable shifts in the legal environment. It wouldn't hurt to keep an eye on emerging legal frameworks and leverage trustworthy resources for updates. So, whether you're analyzing charts or decoding candlestick patterns, remember that being well-informed about regulations can enhance your trading strategy and protect your capital. It's not just about the next big coin; it's about knowing you are making choices grounded in a secure environment. And that, my friends, is a bright picture to aim for as we move forward.

10. The Future of Cryptocurrencies

10.1 Emerging Trends and Technologies

Identifying key trends shaping the future of cryptocurrencies reveals a landscape full of possibilities. One major trend is the increasing adoption of cryptocurrencies by mainstream institutions and retailers, which significantly boosts their market credibility. As more businesses begin to accept digital currencies as a form of payment, the demand for cryptocurrencies is likely to soar. Additionally, regulatory clarity is slowly improving, with more governments crafting frameworks that support and regulate cryptocurrency use. This not only fosters a safer investment environment but also encourages institutional investments, paving the way for a more sustainable cryptocurrency market.

Tailoring investment strategies based on trends in market behavior is essential. For new investors, understanding the fluctuations triggered by technological advancements or market news can help in making informed decisions. Markets have shown they can react sharply to developments from regulatory bodies or innovations in blockchain technology, so staying attuned to these shifts can be a game-changer for budding traders.

Discussing innovative technologies like DeFi and NFTs presents a fascinating chapter in the evolution of cryptocurrency. DeFi, or decentralized finance, offers a new way to engage with financial services, allowing users to lend, borrow, and trade without traditional intermediaries like banks. This democratization of finance is appealing to many, especially the younger generations seeking more control over their investments. Meanwhile, NFTs or non-fungible tokens, have introduced unique digital assets to the market. They enable artists and creators to monetize their work through ownership that cannot be duplicated. As they gain traction, understanding the market dynamics of NFTs becomes crucial for anyone looking to invest. Innovative platforms facilitate trading these assets, offering opportunities for profit but also risks tied to market volatility.

For new investors and traders, navigating this landscape can seem daunting, but education is key. Engaging with community forums, webinars, and thorough reading on both DeFi and NFTs can furnish you with insights that improve your trading acumen. Remember, whether you're looking at stunning candlestick patterns or piecing together the latest in blockchain technology, your journey into cryptocurrency can be as fulfilling as it is financially rewarding. As you venture into these spaces, keeping a finger on the pulse of emerging technologies will stand you in good stead. Stay curious, keep learning, and who knows, you might just find yourself enjoying not only the wilderness of charts but the thrill of exploration as well.

10.2 Predictions from Industry Experts

Gathering forecasts from crypto luminaries and economists about the direction of the market can feel like trying to read the stars while blindfolded. Everyone seems to have an opinion, some backed by serious data, while others appear to be more wishful thinking than hard analysis. Leading figures in the cryptocurrency space, ranging from analysts like Willy Woo to venture capitalists such as Andreessen Horowitz, provide a diverse set of predictions. Some see immense potential in blockchain technology, suggesting that we could see the price of Bitcoin skyrocket into the hundreds of thousands, driven by increasing adoption and institutional investment. Others caution against reading too much into price surges, pointing out the volatility inherent in cryptocurrencies. Understanding who these experts are, and the basis for their predictions, is critical for new investors and traders hoping to navigate this turbulent market.

Understanding varying viewpoints and the rationale behind these predictions involves diving deep into the facts. Some experts may reference past data and trends, explaining how historical cycles can hint at future movements. For instance, the recurring boom-bust cycles of Bitcoin have grabbed attention for their predictability. On the other hand, economists might lean on macroeconomic indicators, discussing how shifts in global finance and government regulations could impact the crypto landscape. It's crucial to consider the underlying motivations of each expert when evaluating their predictions. Those with vested interests might downplay risks or hype possibilities that aren't universally agreed upon. As a new investor, it's wise to sift through the noise and recognize that while predictions can offer guidance, they are still just educated guesses. The objective should always be your informed evaluation of risk versus reward.

Investing in cryptocurrencies requires a solid grasp of chart reading and candlestick patterns, which are essential tools for considering expert predictions. Navigating through the technical indicators and market sentiment can empower you in making more informed decisions. Pair this knowledge with credible resources like reputable crypto news sites, educational platforms, and trusted trading communities. Engaging with others, especially seasoned traders, can also be invaluable. They often have insights that transcend raw numbers and can help illuminate stories behind the data. Remaining skeptical yet open to expert predictions, while reinforcing your learning and trading strategies, can lead to a more balanced and well-rounded investment approach.

10.3 How Crypto Could Transform Finance

Cryptocurrencies have the potential to shake up traditional financial systems in ways that might seem unimaginable right now. Picture this: a world where you don't have to rely solely on banks for transactions and where your money isn't tied to outdated systems that take days to process. These digital currencies let you send and receive money instantly, with lower fees than you'd find in a traditional bank. This could be especially appealing for new investors looking to make the most of their money. Imagine the freedom of having direct access to your funds, without middlemen taking their cut. The democratization of finance through cryptocurrencies is not only possible; it's already happening in various parts of the world. The ability to bank the unbanked is a trendy buzzword these days, but it reflects a real shift where people in underserved regions can finally have access to financial services via their smartphones.

Blockchain technology plays a key role in this transformation. At its core, blockchain increases transparency and efficiency within these systems. Every transaction is recorded on a public ledger that anyone can verify. This means no more shady dealings happening behind closed doors. Fear of fraud decreases when you know that all transactions are out in the open and can be traced back. It's like having a personal accountant who never sleeps, works tirelessly, and always keeps accurate records. This level of transparency could lead to a decrease in corruption, giving customers more trust in financial institutions. Think of how refreshing that would be in today's world! As for efficiency, blockchain can streamline everything from clearing trades to cross-border payments, making them faster and cheaper.

The real kicker is that this technology doesn't just serve the privileged; it extends financial inclusion to everyone, regardless of their socioeconomic status. Imagine being a student just getting started on your investment journey, empowered by a system that welcomes you with open arms instead of daunting barriers. This shift could radically reshape our understanding of finance and investing. Instead of being fearful of the stock market or confused by charts and candlesticks, new traders can engage with a user-friendly, more egalitarian market. With the right resources and guidance, investing no longer feels like an exclusive club; it can become a community. Remember, nurturing curiosity and keeping informed are your best tools as you explore this brave new financial world. If you're curious about where to dive deeper, consider exploring online communities or educational platforms that explain cryptocurrency basics in simple terms.

11. Learning Resources for Crypto Enthusiasts

11.1 Recommended Books and Articles

Building a solid foundation in cryptocurrencies can sometimes feel overwhelming, but there are essential readings that can help clarify the complexities of this digital age. For anyone starting their journey, I recommend The Bitcoin

Standard by Saifedean Ammous. This book isn't just another crypto read; it blends monetary history with the evolution of Bitcoin, offering insights that resonate with both novices and seasoned investors. Another fantastic choice is Mastering Bitcoin by Andreas M. Antonopoulos, which takes a more technical dive into how Bitcoin works. This book is great for understanding the nuts and bolts without feeling like you've enrolled in a doctoral class. For those who lean toward trading, Technical Analysis of the Financial Markets by John J. Murphy provides a wealth of knowledge on charts and indicators, making complex ideas palatable for those looking to day trade or swing trade with crypto assets.

When it comes to articles, websites like CoinDesk and CoinTelegraph frequently publish insightful pieces that cater to new traders and investors. Authors like Laura Shin offer perspectives that are both informed and accessible, breaking down news and trends in a way that empowers readers to make informed decisions. Additionally, "What is Ethereum?" by Vitalik Buterin maintains relevance, especially for newcomers eager to understand the foundational ideas behind smart contracts and decentralized applications. These resources can equip you with the knowledge to navigate the sometimes murky waters of the cryptocurrency market. The important thing is to start soaking in this information; it's all about building a well-rounded understanding over time.

Remember, diving into the world of cryptocurrencies doesn't have to be daunting. It's perfectly fine to take it slow and absorb information at your own pace. Engaging with the community through forums like Reddit or attending local meetups can also complement your readings and articles. Learning from others' experiences can be just as valuable as the books themselves. Always keep a notebook handy; jot down terms or concepts that confuse you. Over time, you'll see progress in your understanding and feel more confident in your investment choices. The key is to stay curious and never hesitate to ask questions—every expert was once a beginner.

11.2 Online Courses and Learning Platforms

Transitioning into the world of cryptocurrency and trading can feel like diving into the deep end without a life jacket. Fortunately, there are excellent platforms that offer structured learning experiences designed specifically for newbies like us. Websites such as Coursera or Udacity provide courses created by experts who break down complex concepts into digestible lessons. These structured paths help you to navigate the vast ocean of information, guiding you through trading basics and crypto fundamentals while offering insights into market behavior. Platforms like Binance Academy or Coinbase Earn not only teach you about cryptocurrency but also provide you with hands-on experiences. Did you know that by completing certain courses on these platforms, you can earn free crypto? It's like being rewarded for learning—who wouldn't want that? Engaging with these resources means you're less likely to fall into the traps that many inexperienced traders do, giving you a solid foundation for your future investing adventures.

One of the biggest advantages of taking online courses is how they streamline the learning process. Instead of sifting through endless articles, YouTube videos, and forums that sometimes feel more confusing than helpful, these courses offer a clear path. You can progress at your own pace, allowing you to absorb the material thoroughly before moving on. This flexibility is perfect for those of us juggling jobs, family, or maybe even just a busy social life. The combination of video lectures, quizzes, and interactive assignments can make learning engaging and fun, making it a lot easier to retain information. Plus, many courses foster a sense of community, allowing you to connect with fellow learners and share insights, tips, and even a laugh or two about the crazy world of trading. It's reassuring to know that you're not in this by yourself, and having that camaraderie can make a significant difference in your learning experience.

For new investors and traders, navigating charts and candlestick reading is a crucial skill. Online courses often break down these concepts into manageable pieces. Having structured lessons is helpful because you can track your progress and revisit challenging topics when needed. This method not only boosts your confidence but allows you to build a comprehensive understanding of how the market operates. A practical tip? When you find a platform or course that resonates with you, stick to it. Consistency is key, and regular practice will ensure that the knowledge sticks. Don't forget to leverage the resources and communities around you. Engage in discussions, ask questions, and you'll discover that the more you immerse yourself in this world, the more naturally it will come to you. So think of it as not just earning badges or certificates, but as building a toolkit full of skills you'll use every day in your investing career.

11.3 Communities and Networking Opportunities

Joining crypto communities can feel like stepping into a bustling marketplace where every conversation is a new opportunity to learn. These communities are where beginner investors find support, and seasoned traders share their hard-earned wisdom. Imagine having a group of like-minded individuals who understand your struggles and celebrate your wins. This is what these communities offer. They are places where questions are encouraged, and knowledge flows freely. In a space as volatile as cryptocurrency, having a network of peers can be a stabilizing force. Whether you're having a tough day in the markets or you just want to understand the latest trends, someone in the community has likely faced similar challenges and can offer insights or even a dose of humor to lighten the mood. The camaraderie found in these groups is invaluable; it's like having a support group dedicated to your financial journey.

To tap into these rich veins of knowledge, new investors need to know where to look. Platforms like Discord, Reddit, and Telegram are teeming with groups dedicated to various aspects of crypto trading. On Discord, for instance, you can find channels focusing on everything from technical analysis to the latest news in the crypto world. Reddit's numerous subreddits related to cryptocurrencies are not only informative but often hilarious, as users share their experiences, both good and bad. Telegram groups can offer real-time updates and a quick way to interact with others in the community. Social media platforms like Twitter also serve as virtual town squares where crypto enthusiasts share tips, memes, and breaking news. Taking the time to explore these forums and engage with the community can provide you with a wealth of knowledge and a sense of belonging that is often missing in traditional investing.

As you dive into these communities, remember that engagement is key. Ask questions, share your insights, and don't be afraid to laugh at your own missteps. Everyone started somewhere, and your experiences could very well help someone else. It's crucial to approach these interactions with an open mind and a sense of humor; markets can be unpredictable, but our ability to connect with others can provide a clearer path through the fog. And here's a practical tip: don't just lurk in the shadows. Be an active participant. You might just find that contributing your thoughts and experiences not only boosts your confidence but also enriches your understanding of the market. Plus, who knows? You might make some lifelong friends along the way.

12. The Psychological Aspect of Trading

12.1 Understanding FOMO and FUD

Fear of Missing Out, or FOMO, and Fear, Uncertainty, and Doubt, or FUD, are two emotions that haunt many traders and investors. FOMO often kicks in when you see others making profits. It makes you feel that if you don't jump in, you'll miss out on a golden opportunity, leading to impulsive decisions like buying stocks at their peak. On the other hand, FUD arises from negative information that clouds your judgment, making you second-guess potential investments. These feelings can lead to hasty trades, driving you to either enter or exit a position before you really understand what's at stake.

The psychological impacts of FOMO and FUD on investors can be profound. For new investors, the excitement of the market can quickly turn cold if they feel overwhelmed by what they perceive as missed chances or looming uncertainties. It might feel like reading a horror story where every twist and turn causes another sleepless night. To manage these emotions, it's essential to ground yourself in rational thinking. Establish a trading plan that includes clear entry and exit points, which helps anchor your decisions. Having a strategy reduces the knee-jerk reactions triggered by FOMO and FUD, allowing you to focus on data rather than speculation.

Being aware of these feelings is just as important as managing them. When you notice that pang of anxiety driven by FOMO or an unsettling notion from FUD, take a step back. Engaging in practices like mindfulness or discussing your concerns with fellow traders can provide clarity. Remember, investing is a marathon, not a sprint, and great opportunities will come around again. Education is your best ally here, so delve into charts, read up about candlestick patterns, and familiarize yourself with various market indicators. Ultimately, the more informed you are, the less susceptible you'll be to emotional trades.

12.2 Managing Emotions in Trading

Maintaining emotional stability while trading in a volatile market is crucial for success. Volatility can push even the most level-headed traders to react impulsively, driven by fear or greed. It's essential to stay grounded and remember your trading plan. One effective strategy is to set clear, predefined limits for loss and gain. When you know beforehand what your limits are, you're less likely to make rash decisions in the heat of the moment. Try to develop a routine that includes regular breaks during trading sessions. Step away from the computer, take deep breaths, and remind yourself that it's just a market—one that often plays tricks on us. It's vital to keep a level head and avoid emotional trading that can lead to regrettable decisions.

Discipline and mindfulness are powerful tools in the world of trading. Incorporating techniques such as meditation and visualization into your daily routine can significantly enhance your ability to remain focused and calm. Picture the trades you want to make and calmly visualize how you will respond to certain market movements. This mental rehearsal can prepare you for the real situations you'll face. Journaling your trading experiences is another step that can help manage emotions. Writing down your thoughts before and after trades not only provides clarity but also helps you reflect on your decisions. Recognizing emotional triggers, whether it's anxiety or overconfidence, can help you create a plan to address them. Remember, trading is not just about numbers and charts; it's also about understanding the emotional rollercoaster that comes with the territory.

Emotional intelligence plays a huge role in trading success. Becoming aware of your feelings can aid in making rational decisions rather than impulsive choices based on fear or excitement. A practical tip is to create a checklist for yourself—a list of things to review when those emotions start to bubble up. Am I sticking to my strategy? Have I reviewed my recent trades? What emotions am I feeling right now? By holding yourself accountable and following through with your plans and practices, you can create a more stable trading experience, making it easier to navigate the ups and downs of the market.

12.3 Building Confidence as a New Investor

Building self-confidence as a new investor often starts with understanding the foundations of investment decision-making. It's like learning to ride a bike; at first, you might feel wobbly and unsure, but with each pedal forward, you gain more balance. One effective strategy is to start small. Invest in areas that pique your interest; that enthusiasm can help you stay engaged and motivated. Taking time to research your investments will also bolster your confidence. Dive into books, reputable financial websites, and market analyses. Discussing strategies with experienced investors or joining forums can provide you with valuable insights. Making a few small, informed investments can help you build a successful track record, which reinforces your confidence. Celebrate your small victories, whether it's acknowledging a well-timed purchase or successfully holding onto stocks during a downturn. Document your decisions in a journal to reflect on what worked and what didn't; this reflection can boost your self-belief over time, transforming past uncertainties into stepping stones for future successes.

Patience is a critical virtue that can significantly enhance your confidence as an investor. The stock market is known for its volatility, and it's easy to feel disheartened by temporary downturns. However, understanding that market fluctuations are normal can help you develop a longer-term perspective. Commit to continual learning and seek resources that will deepen your understanding of market dynamics, such as books, podcasts, or online courses tailored specifically for new investors. Equally important is surrounding yourself with a community of like-minded individuals; this support system can offer encouragement during rough patches and help you to stay grounded. Attend workshops or seminars that focus on investment strategies, and don't hesitate to ask questions. Experience doesn't come overnight, but with patience and a willingness to learn, you'll find that your confidence grows incrementally. Remember, each investment experience adds a layer of knowledge, paving the way for smarter decisions in the future. So, take a moment to appreciate your journey; celebrate the learning curves, knowing that they are essential in nurturing your confidence as an investor.

A practical tip to keep in mind is to set realistic expectations for your investment outcomes. Recognizing that both losses and gains are part of the investment journey can shield you from intense disappointment and help you maintain a more balanced emotional state. Keep reminding yourself that even seasoned investors make mistakes and face losses; it's all part of the game. Embrace this journey with humor and humility, and give yourself grace as you learn and grow. Your confidence will blossom as you navigate the exciting world of investments, leading you to make informed and thoughtful decisions.

13. Case Studies in Crypto

13.1 Success Stories: Big Wins in Crypto

In the world of crypto, success can be as dramatic as a sudden price surge or as steady as a well-planned strategy. Take for example the story of one early Bitcoin investor who bought in at just a few dollars. Fast forward to a few years later, and that humble investment turned into a small fortune, showcasing what can happen when you believe in the potential of technology. Or consider the tale of Ethereum, a project that started small and is now a powerhouse of decentralized applications. The creators had a vision and executed it brilliantly, turning ideas into real-world utility and value.

Success in this space, however, doesn't come by chance. Careful analysis, understanding market trends, and making informed choices are what often set these winners apart. When diving into this volatile market, aspiring investors should pay attention to key factors such as project fundamentals, team credibility, and community engagement. These elements can serve as emotional safety nets when the market feels like a rollercoaster ride. Furthermore, smart risk management and not putting all eggs in one basket can prevent heartbreak. Embrace the volatility but do your research, as the stories of success are not just about being in the right place at the right time but also about being prepared and educated. Develop a clear strategy, stick to it, and let the lessons from the pros guide you through the maze of possibilities.

13.2 Lessons from Failed Projects

Examining notable failures in the crypto space provides a clear lens through which we can view the lessons they impart. Take Bitconnect, for instance. Many were lured in by promises of exorbitant returns, but the reality was a classic Ponzi scheme that left countless investors in financial ruin. The initial allure of easy money blurred many people's judgement. It serves as a poignant reminder that if something sounds too good to be true, it probably is. The downfall of projects like this can teach new investors to prioritize research and due diligence over impulse and hype. Understanding the structural flaws in such projects can save future investors from repeating these mistakes.

Identifying patterns and pitfalls to avoid in future investments becomes crucial after analyzing these failures. Just like in a game of chess, recognizing patterns can mean the difference between winning and losing. Many investors fall into the trap of following trends without understanding the underlying fundamentals. The infamous failure of ICOs in 2018 illustrates this perfectly; many coins launched with no clear purpose or viable technology backing them, resulting in massive losses. Investors should be cautious of overhyped trends and instead focus on educating themselves about a project's utility and the team behind it. Remember that patience is a virtue; take the time to analyze not just what is popular, but what has solid foundations and a clear roadmap to success.

One practical takeaway from these lessons is to diversify your investments and never put all your eggs in one basket. This approach diminishes the risk of significant losses should one project fail. Additionally, consistently educating yourself through credible resources—be it articles, forums, or trusted market analysts—will arm you with the knowledge needed to navigate the volatile landscape of cryptocurrencies. Your financial safety net is built on diligence and continuous learning, so approach each opportunity with both cautious optimism and a healthy dose of skepticism.

13.3 Analyzing Market Patterns through History

Reviewing historical market patterns reveals fascinating insights into the cyclical nature of cryptocurrencies. Throughout history, markets have shown repetitive traits, evolving through phases of speculation, growth, and often, sharp corrections. When you look back at the rise and fall of Bitcoin from 2010 to 2023, you can detect these patterns—phases where euphoria fueled excessive buying followed by periods of fear and selling, creating what we call market cycles. These cycles are not unique to cryptocurrencies but can be found in traditional markets as well. Understanding this dance of emotions—greed and fear—helps new investors recognize that downturns are often just the flip side of a thriving uptrend. Each trend teaches us about the expectations and sentiments of investors, and learning to identify these patterns can equip you with the knowledge to make better trading decisions.

History is an invaluable teacher for shaping future investment strategies. Each major event, from the bubble bursts to unexpected recoveries, whispers lessons that are still relevant today. For new traders, being aware of how past events influenced market behaviors can guide them in crafting thoughtful, informed strategies. For instance, consider the famous 2017 boom—if we analyze that surge alongside its subsequent decline, we can derive principles on timing, emotional discipline, and risk management. It's not about predicting the next big jump but rather recognizing the conditions that foster growth or impending corrections. Arm yourself with insights from historical performance, and you'll find that your investment decisions are likely to be grounded in reality rather than speculation. Approach trading with the mindset that history often repeats itself, allowing you to anticipate potential outcomes while remaining resilient during market fluctuations.

Utilize tools like candlestick charts that visually break down these historical patterns, revealing the intricate dance of buying and selling pressure. The more familiar you become with identifying trends through these visual aids, the more confident you will be when navigating the turbulent waters of cryptocurrency trading. Keep a journal of your trades as well; recording your thoughts and actions encourages reflection, allowing you to learn from both your successes and mistakes. Remember, in the world of investing, patience coupled with a sense of humor about inevitable missteps can provide not only resilience but also growth.

14. Crypto in Everyday Life

14.1 Merchants Accepting Cryptocurrency

Various merchants and businesses are increasingly recognizing the potential of cryptocurrencies, integrating them into their payment systems to cater to a new wave of customers. From local coffee shops to major online retailers, you'll find a range of places where you can now pay with Bitcoin, Ethereum, and other digital currencies. Payment processors like BitPay and Coinbase Commerce are making it easier for these businesses to accept crypto payments, providing necessary tools and support. Even some traditional brick-and-mortar stores are adopting this technology, allowing customers to use digital wallets right at the checkout. Imagine walking into your favorite hangout and paying for your latte with just a swipe on your phone! It's becoming more common and less daunting, which is exciting for both merchants and customers alike.

This trend of integrating cryptocurrency into everyday transactions significantly enhances the viability and acceptance of digital currencies. As more businesses choose to accept crypto, they contribute to its legitimacy and practical use. New investors and traders may find comfort in the growing involvement of reputable companies, which signals that cryptocurrencies are not just a passing fad. It helps bridge the gap between traditional finance and the new digital economy. Additionally, as more people experience the ease and speed of using cryptocurrencies for their purchases, word of mouth spreads, encouraging even more businesses to jump on board. It's a funny twist of fate that something once seen as obscure and risky is now becoming a mainstream option.

For anyone looking to understand this evolving landscape better, focusing on which merchants accept cryptocurrencies can be a game-changer. Observing patterns in adoption will not only help new investors make informed decisions but also give you insight into where the market is heading. So, keep an eye out for those crypto logos next time you're shopping around; it can be an excellent indicator of crypto's road to acceptance in everyday life. If you're new to the game, don't forget to check out platforms like CoinMarketCap or CryptoCompare for resources that can help you navigate your way through the ever-changing market.

14.2 The Role of Crypto in Online Transactions

Cryptocurrencies bring a new level of simplicity to online transactions and cross-border payments. When I first explored the world of digital currencies, I was amazed at how quickly and easily I could send money across the globe. Unlike traditional banking systems, where transfers can take days and involve hefty fees, crypto transactions happen almost instantly. There's something incredibly empowering about knowing that I can send funds to a friend in another country with just a few clicks, all while dodging the convoluted processes of banks and payment processors. It feels liberating, doesn't it? These features stand in stark contrast to traditional methods, which often require navigating through mountains of paperwork and waiting for what feels like an eternity. Moreover, with the rise of blockchain technology, the security it provides adds an extra layer of comfort. Knowing that transactions are immutable and transparent is reassuring for all of us, whether we're new investors or seasoned traders.

When it comes to fees, using cryptocurrencies can be a breath of fresh air. Traditional payment methods often come with hidden costs — think transaction fees, exchange rates, and even fees for receiving funds. With crypto, the fees are typically much lower, especially for international transactions. Every penny saved can go a long way, particularly for students or new investors just starting to dip their toes into the financial waters. Plus, the advantages do not just stop at lower fees. The decentralization of cryptocurrencies means that they are not governed by a single authority, which can lead to less manipulation of prices and more financial freedom. It's refreshing to think that we have options outside of the banking system. Embracing this technology not only opens up new avenues for transactions but also sparks an important conversation about control and ownership in our financial dealings. So, if you're considering how to approach payments in your personal or business life, think about the benefits of using cryptocurrencies. They not only simplify the process but also help you keep more of your hard-earned money.

As you dive deeper into the world of cryptocurrencies, remember to stay informed and do your research. The landscape is continuously changing and presenting new opportunities and challenges. Keep an eye on resources that explain charts, candlestick patterns, and the best practices for investing. For those from older generations or anyone feeling intimidated by the digital shift, humanizing this process through community and understanding goes a long way. You're not alone in this journey—many veterans of the crypto space are eager to share their experiences and wisdom. Embrace curiosity, and you might find that crypto transactions could very well transform your financial interactions for the better.

14.3 Gaining Financial Independence with Crypto

Cryptocurrencies have the potential to empower individuals in their journey toward financial independence and wealth building. For many, the traditional avenues of accumulating wealth feel closed off or too daunting, but the world of digital currencies offers a refreshing alternative. Investing in crypto isn't just for tech-savvy experts or Wall Street moguls; it's an opportunity accessible to all of us. Imagine waking up one day and realizing that your investment has appreciated significantly almost overnight. This isn't just a dream but a reality that countless individuals have experienced with cryptocurrencies. The key is to educate yourself and start with small, calculated risks. Engaging with communities online, watching tutorials, and following market trends can ignite your understanding and confidence, allowing you to navigate this exciting space with greater ease.

Many inspiring stories flood the crypto landscape, showcasing people who have radically transformed their financial situations through this dynamic market. Take Sarah, for instance, a college student who was struggling to pay tuition fees. She started trading small amounts of Bitcoin and, with some diligent research and a dash of luck, turned her modest investment into a scholarship fund. Then there's Dave, a retiree who decided to explore crypto as a way to enhance his fixed income. By investing some savings into altcoins after extensive researching and learning candlestick patterns, he boosted his retirement funds, enabling him to travel the world with his partner. These stories embody the essence of possibility that crypto presents and remind us that although success isn't guaranteed, it is achievable with effort, education, and a bit of strategy.

Understanding that investing in cryptocurrency carries risks is crucial. However, this shouldn't overshadow the potential it holds for financial growth. The critical aspect is to approach it with a balanced mindset. Start by educating yourself on the best resources available. Consider joining communities or forums where discussions about trends, dos and don'ts of the stock market coexist with conversations about crypto. Delve into learning about charts and candlestick reading; these skills can give you an edge in deciphering market movements. Remember, every seasoned investor started somewhere. Approach crypto not just as a financial decision, but as a learning journey. Being curious and proactive can set you apart in this competitive field and lead you towards the financial independence you seek.

15. Conclusion and Final Thoughts

15.1 Recap of Key Takeaways

```html
This book has taken us on quite a journey through the complex world of cryptocurrencies. We've explored various key points that are vital for anyone wishing to navigate this landscape effectively. From the foundational concepts of blockchain technology to the nuanced differences between major coins like Bitcoin and Ethereum, we've unpacked everything you need to know. We've looked at the significance
```

of market trends, the impact of news cycles, and how sentiment can swing prices dramatically within a short period of time. The importance of research stands out, as does the idea that emotional discipline is crucial in trading. Remember, whether you're looking at candlestick charts or traditional stock patterns, the principles remain consistent: knowledge is power, and informed decisions are your best investment strategy.

Investing in cryptocurrencies isn't just about riding the wave of excitement that often accompanies the latest token launch or celebrity endorsement. It's about understanding the underlying technology, the market's inner workings, and the risks involved. This atmosphere can be enticing, especially to new investors or those from generations like Gen X or Boomers, who might be stepping into this vibrant market with fewer tools than younger generations. Playing the long game can yield substantial rewards, and we've emphasized that with the right knowledge and strategies, anyone can become a savvy investor. Always remember that diversifying your portfolio and not sinking all your resources into one asset is a key technique for mitigating risk, allowing you to enjoy the ride without losing sleep.

For those keen to dig deeper, I encourage you to tap into the best resources available, from trusted online forums to educational platforms that cover everything from chart reading to market analysis. Additionally, leverage the wealth of information out there, including webinars, books, and expert interviews. It's also worthwhile to engage with the community – your fellow traders and investors can be a treasure trove of shared experiences. Whether you're just starting out or looking to fine-tune your skills, the crypto world rewards curiosity and knowledge. By staying informed and open-minded, you set yourself up for not just profit, but for a fulfilling journey in the investment landscape.

```
```

15.2 Encouragement for New Investors

Taking that first step into the investing world can feel like standing at the edge of a diving board, heart racing and palms sweaty. But here's the scoop: every successful investor started exactly where you are, filled with questions and nerves. Remember, it's okay to feel hesitant. The key is to embrace that uncertainty and take action anyway. Like trying a new dish at a restaurant—sure, it might seem daunting, but it could lead to your new favorite meal. Empower yourself with the understanding that investing is an opportunity, not just a risk. It's about learning and growing along the way. Your first move may not yield immediate results, but each step offers invaluable lessons that shape your future decisions.

Every investor's journey is wonderfully unique and is akin to a winding maze, filled with colorful opportunities for growth around every corner. That seasoned trader you admire significantly evolved from a rookie who made plenty of mistakes. Those missteps are not failures; they are education opportunities. Just as a painter learns to master their craft through practice and experimentation, you too will uncover your rhythm in the stock market. Embrace your individuality; your experiences will inform your methods and strategies. As you explore different stocks, charts, and candlestick patterns, you will start to develop a sense of what works for you. Look at these experiences as personal growth milestones rather than hurdles. Each investment you make, whether a triumph or a lesson, adds to your unique investment story.

One practical piece of advice for new investors is to keep a journal of your investment thoughts and decisions. Writing down your rationale for each investment, how it performed, and what you learned from it will not only reinforce your understanding but also provide a roadmap of your journey. Over time, you'll see patterns emerge in your thinking and decision-making processes. This reflection can become a tremendous resource as you navigate the sometimes turbulent waters of investing.

Remember, even seasoned investors are still learning. Stay curious, be resilient, and don't shy away from the learning curve—it's what makes this journey worthwhile.

15.3 The Importance of Continuous Learning

In the ever-evolving world of cryptocurrency, the importance of ongoing education can't be stressed enough. Prices rise and fall with such rapidity that keeping up with trends feels like trying to catch smoke with our bare hands. For new investors, traders, and even seasoned individuals dipping their toes into this digital realm, failing to stay informed can lead to costly mistakes. Each day brings new developments, technologies, and market fluctuations that can dramatically shift the landscape. Adaptation is crucial; without it, you're like a ship without a sail, drifting aimlessly amid fierce currents. Continually learning not only keeps you afloat but also helps you navigate toward your financial goals with confidence.

Curiosity should be your best friend. Embrace it wholeheartedly. If something piques your interest or if you encounter a concept you don't fully grasp, dive deeper. There are endless resources available—webinars, online courses, podcasts, and forums buzzing with knowledgeable individuals ready to share their insights. Whether you're a boomer or from Gen

X, there's no age limit on learning. The crypto world is a playground for the curious, and the only stipulation is that you're willing to ask questions and seek out answers. Remember, every expert was once a beginner who didn't hesitate to explore. By cultivating a mindset of continuous learning, you're not just enhancing your investment strategies; you're also setting yourself up for long-term success in an unpredictable market.

As you embark on your journey in crypto trading and investing, immerse yourself in the wealth of knowledge available around you. Make a habit of reading articles or tuning into podcasts about market analysis or candlestick patterns. Each bit of information accumulates, creating a robust foundation for your future decisions. As you learn, you'll grow more comfortable with charts and their intricacies. Harness this knowledge not only to make informed decisions but to instill a sense of empowerment within yourself. Trust me, the more you learn, the more confident you'll feel in your financial decisions, and who knows? That confidence might just lead to your next big win.

www.ingramcontent.com/pod-product-compliance
Lightning Source LLC
Chambersburg PA
CBHW070346230526
45471CB00006B/2444